Kathy's Way

Each day is a gift.
Live it to the fullest.

PETER C. FREIS, MD

ISBN 978-1-0980-1985-3 (paperback)
ISBN 978-1-0980-1986-0 (digital)

Christian Faith Publishing, Inc.
832 Park Avenue
Meadville, PA 16335
www.christianfaithpublishing.com

Printed in the United States of America

Goodness is palpable and attractive. Its magnetic quality and substance permeate the atmosphere. It is tangible and draws you to itself.

Kathy's Message

On November 17, 2018, my wife Kathy, Kathleen Claire Freis, went to Heaven at 7:43 p.m. I share this time rather than the kind physician's time of pronouncement because she grew up in a house numbered 443. This house was a hub about which our family revolved for decades. Four hundred forty-three signified the upbringing Kathy enjoyed, one of faith, beauty, and grace.

Love, beauty, and *grace* describe her wonderfully, but she is more. Saint Francis Cathedral, which seats one thousand people, was filled at her funeral Mass. The Bishop of Metuchen, who never met her personally, knew of her kind and generous life. He called me personally at home to express his condolences and praised her in his correspondence to our family.

Who was she?

Shy Kathy avoided public position, but she participated in everything. She was a quiet, demure little lady who knew how to love. A lesson she taught quietly by example. A lesson we all need to learn. She can still teach us. I know many, many men admire their wives. As caring husbands, they devote themselves to their families, complement and care for them. Yet I know Kathy's ability to love was so special. She possessed a sense of well-being and gratitude. She trusted God. She was free to love. Her love was as spontaneous as taking a breath.

As a loving wife and mother, Kathy prepared in advance all the Christmas gifts for our large family and friends before she entered the hospital in November 2018. I was unaware of these and her other preparations because she shielded me.

Yes, she faced death many times; and again, we, in love with each other, stepped forward. She knew Jesus. She trusted Jesus. She loved Jesus. She trusted Mary and loved her. It was a gift to her that her middle name was after Clare of the Poor Clare Sisters.

She was unafraid. Kathy clung with every breath of her being to continue her life with us on Earth. Her emphatic choice to have surgery as her only option to live still rings in my ears. Seated forward and upright in her chair, she did not hesitate. I can hear her say when offered with choices of therapy, including to do nothing, say "That is not an option."

Who was she?

I first saw her playing on a swing in her backyard at 443 Middlesex Avenue as a child. It was a sunny summer morning. Two young girls with blond hair which glistened in the sun were laughing and playing together. They were enjoying each other while playing on the swings behind a gravel driveway at the side of their home. I watched them shyly from the street side of the hedges for a short time. This was while my father visited a dentist nearby. The girls were so happy and enjoyed playing together. This memory is important even though it relates to her childhood. We grew up to meet and marry each other. Our children played on the same set of swings. Kathy's genuineness was obvious to me from my first glimpse of her playing with her sister.

Love makes you so. This lesson has been taught in my life again and again. God's presence in our life is continuous if we let Him be. Mary's intervention is the same. Both of these realities are very evident in my life experience, personally and professionally. Kathy lived this truth, and I learned it. Imitation is the best flattery. We can all imitate her.

Kathy's faith in Jesus was boundless. She was absolutely correct in trusting God without hesitancy. She knew so well God's limitless love for her and returned it. His love was imitated by her in her every thought, word, and action.

Most of her life, she was tortured by disease. Her life journey was extremely difficult. She persevered, gently, quietly, courageously, beautifully every moment of her life. Her goodness, cuteness, sweetness, and femininity were magnetic. She did everything within her power for our children. Her arms were always outstretched to them. She reached out to everyone. No one was a stranger to her. All were welcome. All were friends. Kathy's friendships were abundantly generous. Even when she could not walk, she found a way to you.

Goodness is truly palpable and very, very attractive. Goodness is inviting. You just want to be in its company. That is who Kathy is. It is that simple. I just always want to be with her.

She was my mother's nurse in late winter 1967. I returned home from medical school to visit my mother in the hospital. At my mother's suggestion, I walked to the nurse's station to meet her. I saw a cute little blond nurse kneeling to retrieve something from a lower cabinet shelf. She returned my greeting. Her pleasing voice and radiant smile said everything. We have shared our life together since that smile.

I consider myself a very, very fortunate man. Left to my own devices, I would not, could not, be as successful without her. Most importantly, I would not be the person I am. Kathy, who loved so easily and well, taught me and many to love. She also invited you to be loved.

Kathy's Way

*T*hank you for your interest in Kathy. Kathy was my wife of nearly fifty years. Not only do I love her, I admire her. She was an extraordinary woman. Her way was a manner and means of making the simple sublime. Kathy elevated ordinary people and place by her attentive presence.

Admiration is truly a high regard for someone, and I admire her as one of the best persons I ever have known. Her amicable nature brought out the best in each person and place. It is worthy of imitation. Few people know her as well as I. We met in our early twenties and defined our life together. We lived a loving marriage built on mutual trust and affection which grew with each moment. We each put the other first.

Why and what did she do so admirably? Her manner was not public or pompous. Her presence was not intrusive. Never seeking to be the center of attention, Kathy always reached out to another. The other person or persons became the focus of attention. This is not an easy task. Why was this her priority? How did she learn to achieve this again and again throughout her lifetime?

Of the many, many people in my life, Kathy was most content. Her contentment permitted her to gift that sense of well-being to those around her. In pain and suffering, her purpose to love gave her the ability to do so.

You cannot give what you do not have. She experienced love in her home. Her family valued closeness. Intimacy is learned in the home. There, there was a peaceful sense of closeness. Kathy made this treasure a part of her and shared it.

Feelings of well-being are essential to overall health and success. Her childhood and past experience shaped her attitudes and outlook on life. Her social, school, and work successes were stepping stones for achievement. Her life's stages rested on a solid stone portal to step forward from.

Kathy was competent and confident. Her life was purposeful; and we drew from our separate experience, our families, and culture to grow. We learned to know and love each other quickly and easily. Soon, we found ourselves planning our wedding and children. We anticipated our family and home eagerly. We were rich but penniless. Our combined efforts enabled opportunity to be realized.

Trust and honesty were essential. Our relationship, our love burst forth and grew. The goals we pursued were similar from the time we met. We joined our hopes and hearts. We wanted vitality, social and personal fulfillment, and a sense of accomplishment. We sought to contribute and make a difference. We wanted to enjoy our children and give them the love and happiness we received.

Kathy and I communicated clearly. Our conversations were friendly and direct. We knew each other and could count on each other. We were accessible to one another. We were free from luxury and complexity. Scholarships and a loan assisted our education, and we earned what we needed. Therefore, we could make our future our way. Those values we did not verbalize were pursued by who we were and what we did. We were a good match. We were a team. Kathy made it all happen!

Kathy's life had a purpose. She purposefully cared lovingly for me, her family, our children, and grandchildren and her extended family as well. Her affection for us energized her. Her affection animated us. Every day was difficult for her because of chronic disease. Kathy suffered with Systemic Lupus Erythematosus. This is a multisystem disease which inflicts pain and disability. She experienced daily pain and discomfort. Each day placed obstacles before her to address. In spite of this, she always loved us and expressed her love. If you met her, you would not see, and she would not offer any evidence of her trial. Her caring was her prayer. In loving us, she loved God.

Kathy's caring influenced people for the better. She was an extraordinary woman who lived an extraordinary life. She utilized the everyday routine to advantage.

Her faith, lived not preached, sustained her. Faith in God, His love, and the sacraments nourished her. We married with a Mass fully committed to a lifetime together. Her values and ability to love were the attributes that welcomed you to her. These qualities formed a bond between you. Everyone who grew to know her recognized her goodness. I continue to see and meet numerous people who praise her as soon as we say hello.

Goodness is palpable and attractive. Its magnetic quality is inviting. Its substance permeates the atmosphere. Goodness is tangible and draws you to itself.

The possession of these salutary attributes facilitates a demeanor that is peaceful. Contented, humble, and willing to learn, the individual can offer genuine affection through empathy and kindness. It seems, if you are at ease with yourself, you can be comfortable with others. You can comfort regardless of the circumstances. My wife dealt with postoperative pain, lupus, loss, grief, or hardship successfully. The agony did not pass from sight. She reached out to those around her, particularly if there was a need to address. Conflict or cooperative interactions are workable. She demonstrated what a person can do regardless of their personal reality. Problems can actually be productive. You can profit from any experience. Each encounter can nurture. At a town fundraiser for medical care, Kathy was in touch by phone and opined, "God can make good come out of anything." Perhaps that is what loving is all about, the blossoming of the goodness within each of us. Kathy nourished the people in her life very well.

In the brief recitation of small portions of her life, the reader may observe, really witness, and understand the telling influence of Kathy's presence. Her presence served to edify and to uplift relationships.

Kathy was a joy to be with. She was whole and wholesome, pretty and petite, a giant and a hero. My wife was my friend and my soulmate. She was a worker and a playmate, a friend who was a gentle critic, who provided an example to follow. Hers was a gentle, supportive voice to be heard. When she sang, her music was beautiful, soft and gentle to the ear.

Interested and interesting, she was a wonderful companion. Wise in her thought and words, her advice was always beneficial. In her wisdom, Kathy knew when not to speak. When she spoke, her words guided the thought and the conversation or the activity at hand. She always made a contribution. Elegant while simple, her person and presence were a constant joy.

She knew you better than you knew yourself. Capable of surprising the listener with the detail of her observation, Kathy taught. She truly educated.

Very modest, her honesty augmented her action and word. Kathy would accept a compliment graciously or a criticism with appreciation. Each day was better because she was there.

Each task, each game, each relationship grew. Every challenge, each impossible task was quietly approached with determination. Kathy's illness, pain, and suffering were a part of most of her life. These were all anticipated, met, and endured with one goal, to love us all.

Perhaps learning a little bit about Kathy will be of benefit. I hope so. Her purpose in life was to love and care for others. Her love was explosive. It was penetrating and permanent. My life, because Kathy became my wife, the mother of our children and grandchildren, is the best it can be. She is my best friend. I am a better person because of her. I see her wonderful presence and traits in our children.

My hope is to continue her message and convey her lessons. She is an example of how to love and accept love. Kathy would look at you lovingly, smile, and thank you while she expressed her appreciation for your attention in word or action.

In appreciation and gratitude for my wife, I thank you.
God bless you.

Kathy's guy,
Pete

Kathy's Story

*K*athy's story is a narrative that needs to be told. It is a journey worthy of retelling and remembering. Her story merits attentiveness and awe. Kathy's kind, tender, solicitous, understanding, and sympathetic manner demands imitation.

My spouse's message is so genuine that I want to share it. She cannot speak to us at the moment, but her life and smile can still be appreciated and heard through the warm reception of her message.

Kathy's journey was not easy. In fact, it was unimaginably difficult. Talented and motivated by love, she persevered. She pushed forward quietly, gently, courageously, beautifully every moment of her life. Her goodness, cuteness and femininity were attractive.

Yes, I am in love with her. So is every person who knew her.

My reason for telling you about Kathy is to demonstrate how much each of us can do just by being the person you are. By being herself, she inspired the good in others. This is a wonderful accomplishment. Her simply, completely genuine idealistic nature was defined by love. Our mutual confidence and trust was empowering. It offered a lifetime of contentment. She alone possessed a wholeness and clarity in her person that was unequalled.

The Poandl Family

The Frank and Dorothy Poandl family were well known in Metuchen, New Jersey. They were active in their parish and appreciated for their generous and genuine giving of themselves. Theirs was a busy home. It was an honest, warm, safe, and comfortable home. Her home was the gathering place for extended family when she was a child. Her education started one block away.

She attended Saint Francis School and then Metuchen High School a short half mile from home. She followed her dream of caring for others through Saint Francis School of Nursing in Trenton, New Jersey.

Extremely capable, she mastered the school's accelerated nursing program. After graduation, she exercised her clinical skills at Saint Peter's Hospital in nearby New Brunswick, New Jersey, where I met her.

Kathy was the fourth child, one of ten children. Elizabeth, Robert, and Patricia were her seniors. They were her playmates in the beautiful yard at 443 Middlesex Avenue in Metuchen. Her younger siblings enjoyed the spacious property as well. I did also.

When we dated and in subsequent years as well, we were in the yard constantly. Something was always happening. It was the meeting place.

When her brothers and sisters were young, we played together. Baseball, football, and volleyball enlivened the day. All generations participated. Sometimes the competition was intense. Neighbors joined in. It was a generous size yard allowing for tons of fun. There was a full two-hundred-fifty feet behind the home, and the yard stretched to a back street, Highland Avenue. It was a site that hosted the family and very large party crowds. It was the location of birthdays, anniversaries, Easter egg hunts, and countless barbeques. Four forty-three was a favorite spot. It was so for decades and multiple generations.

Four forty-three, its affectionate name, was home. Metuchen was where Kathy and I returned to raise our growing family. We purchased a home just a little more than a block away from 443. Kathy's parents resided at 443 Middlesex Avenue. It was a very short walk to Grandma's and Grandpa's home We returned home to Metuchen when we completed our military service. We planned to raise our family with their grandparents to cherish. My mother lived a short distance from us as well. My father passed away just a few months before unexpectedly when we were on active duty with the US Army. We needed to be home.

Metuchen was where Kathy was nurtured. Her family home was there. My family was there. It was truly home. There is a comfort in being home. It is a place to refresh and refuel. It is the doorway to the life we live.

Metuchen is a two-mile square oasis in central New Jersey. This tiny town is a refuge from the hectic pace and uneasiness of life. My mother was born there. An uncle was mayor. Another relative, Reverend White, was pastor of the Presbyterian Church. My grandfather camped in the Woodwild, which is an ecologically preserved woodland, with Mayor Nate Robins. The address 443 Middlesex Avenue was the Nate Robins Estate.

Today that site is a small remnant of its earlier size. The property has shrunk to 1.1 acres over decades. This was a small fraction of its original size. The one-hundred-years-plus home was divided into apartments after World War II. This restructuring of the house provided homes for military personnel returning home from the war. The renovated majestic Robins Estate continued to be warm and inviting.

Kathy's attractiveness, sweetness, and warmth came from home. She learned how to love from her family, her Catholic tradition, and supportive social culture.

All three united in her perspective, thoughts, feelings, and actions. Her way of living was really her faith in action. Faith can grow. Families become larger.

This mini-family fan club grew as our family grew. Everyone in each generation was invited to the club. We enjoyed being family. We were Yankee fans. Over the years, we enjoyed many baseball games at Yankee Stadium. We attended as a crowd, including our daughters, their husbands and children.

Kathy's Dad and I attended Yankee games together when, as a physician in training, I was privileged to provide care to the fans at Yankee Stadium. This affiliation permitted us years later to bring a much older Grandpa Frank Poandl to meet the team at the stadium as a Yankee guest. The players of both teams were wonderful. Each of the athletes and some of their spouses and a few of their children met Dad and greeted us. It was a win for everyone!

Play, Shall We Dance?

*W*e had a lot of fun together and laughed with joy often. We ran. We played ball, and we loved to dance. We spent every moment we could together. Dancing was the most fun.

Actually we were in step with each other from the moment we met. At home, on the dance floor, regardless of the tempo, we blended gracefully together. In each other's arms, we glided across the dance floor. We enjoyed the music and its story. Our dances throughout our lifetime are captured in our hearts. We could lead each other, and we anticipated every step. The pulse of the music was ours. Kathy and I danced like we lived, as one. Our dance was sheer happiness. We were content.

Special events, such as weddings and parties, were invitations to the dance floor. They were enthusiastically accepted. Those attending often recognized our enjoyment and stopped their dance to watch us. This allowed us to share our fun with them. The smiles and laughter afterward cemented all of us happily together with memories to cherish.

Many forms of dance, including square dancing, brought friends and family closer. Each wedding over the years and generations offered a new genre. We joined in.

Something new was an invitation. Ballroom dance lessons with other couples were a chance to laugh and learn together. "Always together" is a theme for couples and their community to mold their trademark. Togetherness promotes happiness.

A dance is an opportunity to bring people closer. There is a true camaraderie that dancing brings about. Music lightens the atmosphere. The cheerfulness created bonds between us all. It beckoned us back. We returned to the dance floor again and again. We were a dance team. Actually we were a true-life team, truly partners.

Kathy and I had many invitations to dinner, sporting events, picnics, and plays. Of interest, even fanciful academic or business galas rose from a possible staid evening to one of enjoyment with Kathy. Yes, dancing was included.

We have warm memories of visits to the homes of friends and family throughout all of our over fifty-two years together. Friendships were made when we were students and through our own children when they attended school. There was always an opportunity to volunteer at school, church, or in the community.

As newlyweds, our little group of friends were all married while we were in medical school. We gathered in our new homes. We lived in tiny apartments or houses. Everyone counted their pennies.

Students all, our wives would prepare delicious but simple meals. New husbands, we would attempt to barbeque on apartment balconies. Most of all, we chatted constantly about anything. We were good friends who enjoyed each other. We possessed common goals.

Our group was assembled from the entire breath of our country. We were different in many ways. We were all also caring people who shared the goal of caring for others.

The friends we made returned to their homes after completing their education, home to join their families of origin. We did the same.

Most of the new couples rented apartments. I really wanted a little house with a yard to rent. While anticipating our marriage in six months, I worked in the chemistry laboratory of DC General Hospital. I then lived in a hospital-provided housing as pay for my employment.

Students from all three medical and some of the dental schools in the Washington DC area shared quarters. We were a good group who worked well together. In that setting, one evening, I saw an ad for a house in Arlington, Virginia, for rent. It became our first home.

Our first home, which I rented after seeing it once at night, was a cinder block two-bedroom cottage. I saw it once at night on a break from the lab. I described it glowingly to Kathy by phone. She believed my description.

It was built to house Pentagon employees during World War II. It was sort of an okay for a start. Far from what she expected, Kathy went to work. She really must have loved me. Once we moved in, I readily realized its limitations.

Without complaint, she made it our home. I loved the yard and enjoyed mowing it while Kathy worked at the hospital. She was the head nurse on Two South which was a medical floor at the George Washington University Hospital. She made everything better.

We enjoyed our Arlington home and grilled in the backyard. It was a place to relax. We worked hard. Family visited often. She was a good host. We soon learned that our little house would be inadequate.

While visiting for a few days, my mother was informed that the house would be very cold in the coming winter. A neighbor told her of the anticipated discomfort. We made plans to move. We were expecting our firstborn.

The same friends we joined for fun and food came to our assistance. Bill, Tom, Chuck, and I, all GW medical students whitewashed the house and raised the rent ten dollars. This allowed us to break the lease. Kathy and I were free to move to a warmer nearby apartment building. Once more, Kathy took things in stride. We welcomed our baby girl to a nice cozy warm home.

It was there that Kathy gave me my first graduation party. Our family and all of her family came from New Jersey. What a wonderful day. She always made me feel special. Kathy gave everyone her generous heart. She was inexhaustible.

We had to be tireless. So much had to be done daily. It was easy to laugh together. The Lord blessed us with two more gorgeous little girls in the next two busy years. They were beautiful. We were thrilled. Our love for them was limitless.

Carolyn attended my graduation and the party. Patti joined us for our first fall and Christmas back in New Jersey. Theresa was born eleven months later. They all marched into military service when I reported for active duty.

All of this craziness was still delightfully happy. Kathy made it so.

There Are Many Ways to Lead a Life

*T*here are many ways to lead your life. The choices of a lifetime are powerful. Choices have consequences. Turns in the road not only offer new direction, but each turn follows the former. We learn from the past and create our future.

Education is lifelong. We are social beings who need each other. Home, school, and playground are classrooms. As infants, our social experience teaches us our identity. We learn to respond to the expressions and mannerism of those who are handling or holding us. Observation tells us what behavior works or does not. Reward breeds success. Negative experiences are an opportunity to learn. We grow and mature. Our childhood experiences of life prime our values and goods. We internalize values as we grow. We conceptualize values. Goals are pursued, and promises are kept as we mature.

In adolescence, the understanding of the concepts of truth and goodness is possible. When the individual internalizes a value, it can become a goal to achieve or acquire. A rule enforced on an individual can be internalized as meritorious, and the desired behavior followed without external supervision. The qualities of kindness and selfless-ness alter our behavior, particularly so in relationships. Experience can be an event that reinforces or contradicts our values. Either, experience is an opportunity.

Kathy and I grew up in homes of limited financial means, but we were rich. We were loved. Dorothy and Frank Poandl loved their ten children immeasurably. Kathy was their fourth child and third daughter. She played and grew up in the house we would return to. We returned home after seven years and bought 443 for Kathy's parents. Gratitude for their generous love was what motivated us. Gratitude is a source of comfort which you can build on.

It was a pleasure to meet her family. I met her younger siblings as children and young teenagers. Each of them mirrored the affection showered on them in their home. Each gave it away. They, parents and children, possessed the warmth I felt in Kathy. It was just a pleasure to be with her then as now. I just want to be with her.

We returned home to Metuchen and our children attended the same St. Francis School Kathy attended. I always thought it was one way to give them their identity, a way to support who they were and where they came from. We all need to know who we are.

Ordinary People Do Extraordinary Things

*O*rdinary people do extraordinary things every day.

We all complete mundane tasks of cooking and cleaning, putting out the garbage, and, when exhausted, finish one more leftover task before falling asleep. The next morning greets us with a similar list of things to do.

This agenda can include the choice of how to complete the ordinary. This tightly packed list can be made purposeful and productive. Yes, it can be made enjoyable and rewarding. If not personally, it can reward another. You might choose to prioritize why you would get out of a cozy warm bed on a rainy Monday morning. You define what motivates you.

In college, a very cogent and compelling professor would say that God loved ordinary people because He made so many of them. He was correct.

We meet many ordinary people, many anonymous, every day. They provide for us behind the scenes. These people may be invisible but instrumental to our well-being, perhaps essential to our well-being.

It is very obvious to me that there are many good, wonderful, loving people throughout the world, moms and dads, kids and grandparents, friends and fellow workers. Students, teachers, young and old, all come in many wonderful varieties. They teach us and care for us by their loving touch.

I know there are many, many fortunate husbands. Countless couples raise each other as individuals and as a couple to unattainable heights. This would be impossible without their love for each other. Matrimony is empowering. The sacrament gifts each spouse to the other. Marriage begins in love, matures through love, is sustained by love, forgives through love. It is grace filled and gifting.

As a means of encouragement, I have repeatedly told exhausted mothers that moms go straight to heaven. I add the wish that they leave the door slightly ajar for fathers.

Our values and close relationships are experienced and learned in the home. Intimacy is essential to well-being. The social skills necessary for a close relationship are acquired in the home. It is where our story begins, a common quotation.

Each of us has a purpose and a message, a story to tell, a life to share. We will all do it differently. Each of us is an individual. We all possess unique attributes that define us. These characteristics and values molded by experience shape one's perspectives.

Our family and community comprise a small world, which grows as we grow. Horizons expand and fill us with widening perspectives. The natural curiosity of a child can continue as we mature so that we may never stop learning.

Learning has social and academic sides. We can learn different lessons from positive or negative experiences. Our feelings influence our thoughts. Our ideas influence our emotions. Our response to either can be chosen or unthinking.

Personal values are the product of our education and experience. Our education begins as an infant in our home and continues there. Outside the home, in multiple academic settings, we add to our social repertoire.

I believe this to be an essential process to well-being. We reject and accept the values presented to us from many sources as we age. This process during one's youth is defining. We convey who we are and what we value in our play, work, and relationships. Our internalized values crystalize our self-perception. It also defines our vision of other people and the world. In the small world of our youth, we still affect others. Our influence expands to others and affects the world as a whole. These values mold our relationships and the legacy we bequeath. We convey ourselves in our family, our children, our friends, and community.

To be healthy and to give health, some attributes are fundamental. Past physical or emotional experiences affect our attitudes and outlook by the manner in which they impact our perception. The choices or lack of choices we made in response are consequential. Positive values of dedication, devotion, loyalty, faithfulness, fidelity, attentiveness, and allegiance are fruitful.

I believe these values, among others, are abundantly widespread. Ordinary people accomplish extraordinary things.

Kathy and I

Kathy and I were an ordinary couple doing ordinary things. We enjoyed the summer outdoors. Boy Scouts activities with her younger brothers offered the opportunity to go to the foothills of the Allegheny Mountains in northwestern New Jersey. The scouts brought you to rural parts of the state. The trips were fun and fruitful.

One Sunday, the summer before our formal engagement, we enjoyed a Sunday afternoon ride. There was no particular destination and no hurry.

New Jersey Route 206 travels north-northwest toward Pennsylvania. It offers beautiful scenes, and it is dotted with a variety of small house-bound stores. These cottage industries include outdoor unfinished furniture.

We stopped to look, not truly shop. But we purchased an unfinished cradle and brought it home. We wanted a family and cherished children. Postponing a family was not an option either of us wanted.

Our formal engagement would be six months away. There were years of training and a military obligation to face. Although we would still be in medical school, we had confidence in our future. Confident and comfortable in our decisions, even though we were penniless, we planned to make it all happen. We did. My father asked, "What is that for?" when he saw the cradle.

I answered, "A baby."

Many newborns rested in the cradle. Our children, Carolyn, Patricia, Theresa, Beth, Sean, and Kevin spent their first months sleeping snuggly inside. Many of our grandchildren did as well. To prepare its wood and finish, was not a task. It was fun. I also finished a crib, which was handed down from Kathy's older sister and our nieces and nephew all slept in it. We finished the cradle in the basement of our apartment to welcome our children. Kathy and I were thrilled to anticipate our children.

Younger than me but wiser, she found pleasure and happiness in the moment. She did so enthusiastically. That was and is attractive in her. This simple patience and active involvement in the moment continued throughout her life. Kathy was easy to be with, to be near.

When dating, we did simple things. Rides, walks, talks, movies, and the beach filled our days. So many couples do. Contentment describes the pleasure of being in her presence. She was a practicing nurse who came from a large loving family. She was well aware of the future demands, as well as its happiness. I had a lot to learn. I learned well from her example.

As medical students, we rotated through specialties in groups of four students. This comprised the last two years of formal training before being awarded your degree. The formal September-through-May academic calendar ended. While on clinical rotations, the students were permitted an eight-week break, which was assigned randomly. Three of the four people I rotated with were planning their own weddings. Through mutual cooperation, we arrived at dates for the marriages. I was free in February and March of 1969. Engaged on January 20th, 1968, we planned the ceremony for February 16, 1969. It was fun to plan our future. We were starting our own life and eagerly anticipating every part of it.

We accepted each other as individuals who would place mutual trust in each other for a lifetime. Trust was so very much alive and easily accepted. My wife-to-be knew starting our marriage in school would be challenging. She knew better than I the details of creating a home and family. She also knew that I had a military obligation to fulfill after my formal education. I had been a student my whole life. She was a professional.

In my junior year of college, I enlisted in advanced Army ROTC. I was preparing for medical school and dropped out of the program only to realize through the newspaper coverage of the Vietnam War that I would certainly serve in the military. I enlisted and, in conversation with the professor of military services, jokingly related that perhaps I could intern in Hawaii! I also was aware that I had to pay for my education.

This was serious business. I knew I wanted a family of my own. My own family filled my heart with wonderful warm memories.

Cousins and friends frequented our home. Sunday Mass followed by a big breakfast was only to be undone by Mom's Sunday dinner. The evening brought family together for another meal. A favorite was open-faced broiled cheese sandwiches, sometimes topped with tomatoes.

Kathy loved these also, and we included these in our family menu. When she was unable to prepare a dinner, the open-faced cheese sandwiches tided us over. She was the best cook. I knew she would be when I sampled her second-to-none eggplant parmesan early on while I was getting to know her.

The Struggle

*K*athy suffered for years because of systemic lupus erythematosus. It robbed her of enjoyment, mobility, and years of the everyday pleasures we all enjoy. The disease stole our children as part of its early presentation with five miscarriages. It kept her from her home. The disease dominated her and demanded total control of her. Her courageous spirit said no. She resisted through abdominal and heart surgery, heart attacks, cardiac catheterizations, sepsis, pneumonia, immunotherapy, radiation therapy, chemotherapy, an autologous stem cell transplant, arthralgia, abdominal pain, and daily with her malaise. Determination described her. Patience did also. Without complaining or asking, "Why me?" she still reached out. She looked after her family. She ached for them when apart.

The name *lupus* very well describes the character of the disease as a predator.

Lupus is:

- Painful
- Cruel
- Relentless
- Destructive
- Persistent
- Consuming
- Threatening
- Ever-present
- Lurking
- Stalking

- Shackling
- Imprisoning

Ms. Mary Jean Irion's excerpt which was on a wall in our home read:

> Normal day, let me be aware of the treasure you are. Let me learn from you, love you, bless you before you depart. Let me not pass you by in quest of some rare and perfect tomorrow. Let me hold you while I may, for it may not always be so. One day I shall dig my nails into the earth, or bury my face in the pillow, or stretch myself taut, or raise my hands to the sky and want, more than all the world, your return.

Kathy placed it where it would readily be seen because our daughter, like her, was a victim of another connective tissue disease, scleroderma. She required major surgery. Both of them suffered. Both are absolutely beautiful. All of our children directly, or indirectly, bore the pain. All are beautiful people who know love and know how to love. You cannot carry a burden of this magnitude alone. God loves us.

I taught rheumatology with an excellent rheumatologist, outstanding in her field. One day, she gently advised a young woman with devastating disease of her therapeutic options. The patient was an older teenager who was severely ill. Systemic lupus erythematosus was robbing her of her life. The outstanding clinician, by her education and clinical acumen, first offered the young woman her therapeutic options. The doctor then stated, "And lupus will take you where it will."

Lupus stalks its victims. The name is derived from ancient descriptions of its lesion as resembling a wolf's bite.

The wolf was always at our door. Sometimes out of sight, it would return in a more vicious state.

We enjoyed good health together the first five years of our marriage. We were the proud parents of three daughters and very busy, busy with the completion of medical training and military service. The demands were huge but met happily together with determination.

We worked. We played. The company of friends and family enlivened our lives. Kathy was an unofficial tour guide of Washington DC, New York City, and West Point, New York. The tourist sites at each location became a pleasant day or weekend followed by equally pleasant memories. If I worked, Kathy was the escort until I could meet the party. It was great to be with family and friends.

Sunday rides to Williamsburg or the Blue Ridge Mountains in Virginia brightened our days. I can still picture playing with our child in the grass of Manassas in the summer. We would celebrate Christmas twice, first out of state and again back home. Santa was generous.

We would host our siblings or visit my brother's family, who was stationed in a nearby military post, bearing melted ice cream in the summer heat.

Later in these years, Kathy experienced abdominal pain. Her medical needs were addressed. She was treated and improved, but no firm diagnosis was achieved. We continued with the day's routine and accepted all invitations, even when she was uncomfortable. Finally we settled in back home in New Jersey and really enjoyed being at home.

Jogging, dancing, and energetic gleeful play with our now four children occupied each day. We ran three miles daily. Kathy started our daily jog while we were at West Point. She always loved to run. The joy of running continued for years. Our girls ran with us. When too young to participate, they watched and played while they waited. We made it all a game. Our oldest girls ran cross country in high school and college. We ran along. Our sons played soccer, basketball, and baseball.

We did not understand the whisper of disease that was to shatter our life. We conceived and lost our children. Medical evaluation did not fully explain the cause in spite of comprehensive care. The abdominal pain returned more severe and more frequently than before.

Still without allowing evidence of her distress, Kathy participated in everything. Her ceramic artistry still graces homes from coast to coast. As Kathy's discomfort and diminishing immunity became more profound, she did not complain. As always, she readily invested herself in each day. She participated in people's lives. Our daughter told us Mom taught her children to participate in people's lives. She said she is following her example.

She took sewing classes, which led to her becoming an accomplished seamstress. In demand, her sewing skills were sought. Her accomplishments benefited others. Her Halloween costumes, beautiful dresses, blouses and slacks were popular.

A long Hawaiian dress she fabricated for a dinner dance and a polka dot dress she made to place my new rank on my shoulder when I was in the military stand out. The Hawaiian kimono-like robe was matched by my formal dress shirt by Kathy. Her talent was admired, inviting our friends closer.

In spite of the obstacles of illness, Kathy was involved. She continued to sew. Her ceramic Christmas trees and praying Santas grace the homes of at least three generations. She stepped outside our home.

She became an EMT. Kathy served as the president of the Metuchen Safety Council. She was the copresident of the home school program and printed school papers for the elementary school teachers for decades. Of course, she was a soccer mom, cheerleading mom, basketball, cross-country, track, and baseball fan for all of our six children. Nine grandchildren were cheered for as well.

When the wolf, lupus erythematosus, was at our door, everything changed. When SLE came home, its impact was unimaginable. Encompassing every aspect of our life, the disease insidiously stepped in. Smoldering and bubbling up, its tide splashed suddenly into our eyes. It stung our skin and plunged deeply into our being. The disease touched our souls. The disease defined most of our lives and is much of our history. It scars and leaves footprints.

Footprints tell a story. Left by all, as we tread on life's path, the print left behind tells its owner. Footprints are recognizable. Steps can be shallow or deep. Each can vary by stride or size. Footprints can demonstrate a group or solo being. Our steps can demonstrate a reaction or a beginning. Regardless, the impact is significant. Its consequences are determining. Our footsteps may be a metaphor for our lives. What do they say? What legacy did or will we leave?

The imprint of lupus was recognized in 1993. Kathy was definitively diagnosed with SLE. The telltale malar rash on her face coupled with her abdominal pain, painful joints, and the malaise produced by sunlight confirmed her disease.

How do we address this? How do we live with this? Her answer was to quietly, purposefully go on as a beautiful wife and mother. She was comfortable in persevering because she was courageous.

Fortunately our medical and nursing educations were very supportive of our needs. Actually, our educations were invaluable. My introduction to SLE was in pathology during my first years of medical school. I was bewildered at the concept of a disease that was the manifestation of the body attacking itself. Throughout my career, I have studied SLE.

We needed help. We needed a lot of help. Kathy was suffering with severe abdominal pain and joint pain. She lost weight. She could not eat.

Diagnostic efforts were extensive but indeterminate. She had surgery and more testing of the blood vessels in the alimentary tract was diagnostic. The superior mesenteric artery, a large vessel supplying the intestine, was inflamed. This vasculitis dominated her life. Chemotherapy for years followed by an experimental stem cell transplant quieted the disease. Her rescue was costly. The late manifestation of connective tissue disease can be cardiac. Her heart was challenged.

My wife endured over seventy cardiac catheterizations because of recurring blood vessel occlusions in her heart. Actually the sentinel blood vessel was in her abdomen, destroying the abdominal organs.

She survived after chemotherapy and an experimental autologous (her own cells) bone marrow transplant. The stem cell transplant left her susceptible to many infections.

Constant vigilance and care were fruitful but limited. Her breast cancer of many years was in abeyance. The periodic surveillance for the breast cancer explained the new abdominal pain which awakened her four months before her death. A second cancer, adenocarcinoma of the pancreas, required major surgery. The removal of the cancer was successful. But the surgery required removal of important intestinal blood vessels. This made Kathy dependent on the aged and damaged vessels which were destroyed by the SLE.

She wanted to live. She chose to live just as she had multiple times before. She wished to live and love, regardless of the struggle. Kathy hoped to stay with us. She was always a part of us.

Only once I asked Kathy, "How do you feel when you feel well?"

She answered, "When I feel well, it is like you feel when you have the flu."

I was and I am still speechless to know this. Kathy personifies courage and grace-filled character. Her demeanor and silent simple posture suggested a comfort and ease which was not present. She kept her pain a secret.

Still, Kathy's ability to join in any activity was admirable. She jumped in and participated. She did her part and shared another's effort. The ability to see what interested someone else was an invitation to her.

She shared the event, the interest, the task, and those things valued by the people present to her in whatever way. She shared her enjoyment with you in return.

When at a theme party, mutual compliments were always exchanged, the pleasure of each other's company was enhanced. Her warm way of sharing, listening, and joining in was so natural to her. It was as automatic as breathing.

Her manner benefitted us all. She, in exchange, gained a friend and enhanced a relationship. Her temperament and disposition were always pleasant and inviting.

Kathleen Freis

METUCHEN - Kathleen C. Freis, 71, of Metuchen died on Saturday, November 17, 2018 at the Hospital of the University of Pennsylvania in Philadelphia, PA.

Born in Newark, she was a lifelong Metuchen resident. Kathy was a lifelong communicant of St. Francis of Assisi Cathedral in Metuchen. She was a graduate of St. Francis School of Nursing in Trenton. She worked as a registered nurse in both New Jersey and Washington D.C., before retiring from St. Francis Cathedral School.

She was devoted to her family, proudly wearing the crown of wife, mom, and grandma.

She was predeceased by her parents, Frank and Dorothy Poandl, as well as two sisters Elizabeth Breen and Carol Trecolis and brother in law Peter Trecolis.

Surviving are her husband of 49 years Dr. Peter C. Freis; four daughters Carolyn DeMaio (Christopher), Patricia Ackerson (Richard), Theresa Freis, Elizabeth Freis-Blom (Thomas); two sons Sean and Kevin Freis; her siblings Fr. Bob Poandl, Patricia LaPointe (Jerry), Tom Poandl (Debbie), David Poandl (Pam), Edward Poandl (Diane), Tina Soliman (Yasser), and William Poandl (Mary Beth); a brother in law Jim Breen; ten grandchildren: Joseph (Kristina), Marc, Briana, Christa, Cara, Joshua, Kyle, Jacob and Leila. She is also survived by many nieces and nephews.

Services will take place on Saturday, November 24, 2018 at 9:45 AM from the Costello-Runyon Funeral Home 568 Middlesex Ave. (RT 27) Metuchen, followed by a 10:15 AM Mass of Christian Burial at St. Francis of Assisi Cathedral, interment will follow at Resurrection Burial Park in Piscataway. Visitation is Friday from 4-8 PM. In lieu of flowers or donations, please use your time and money to go out and play with your children and grandchildren, because that is what Kathy would want. That is how she and Pete have lived every day.

To send condolences please visit costello-runyon. com.

Nursing School
She graduated in 1966

This photo was a gift to me after our engagement
with her pledge "all my love forever".

Feb. 16, 1969

A FAMILY PRAYER

Heavenly Father, thank you for the gift of our family. Enlighten our hearts and minds that we may live more fully this vocation to love.

In our daily life and work,
may we reflect the self-giving love which you,
O Father, eternally show with your Son
and the Holy Spirit.

Let your love be evident in the peace that reigns
in our home and in the faith we profess and live.
May our family always be a place of generosity,
understanding, forgiveness and joy.

Kindly give us the wisdom and courage
to be witnesses to your eternal design for
the family; and grant that the Holy Family
of Nazareth may always guide our path
to holiness as a family.

We ask this through our Lord Jesus Christ,
your Son, who lives and reigns with you in the
unity of the Holy Spirit, one God forever and ever.
Amen.

 Prayer composed by Archbishop William E. Lori of Baltimore, Supreme Chaplain. The cover image of the Holy Family is a drawing by Giovanni Balestra, based on a painting by Sassoferrato. The original print is housed at the Pontifical John Paul II Institute for Studies on Marriage and Family in Rome. Used with permission.
10085 1-14

We prayed this prayer nightly.

Our Wedding Day

Married less than a month we visited
Kathy's brother Bob in Mississippi March 1969

Sean, Beth, Carolyn, Kathy, Pete, Patti, Theresa, Kevin.
Our six children

Mom and Dad,

Today we're here to remember and celebrate the 25 years of your lives together. Many of these years we've been lucky enough to share with you, because we exist as a result of your love. Throughout these years, your love has brought us so many things that each of us will cherish forever, and that will allow us to have higher expectations, more value for life's little things, and constant hope that we CAN be better and make a difference in this world. Thank you for being the best example of immeasurable love, generous and steadfast, in a world where it sometimes seems not to exist.

Thank you:

For our family vacations. You always made it a point to include everyone and make time for family fun.

For making each and every holiday and birthday as special and unique as the first, even if it meant staying up all night.

For being the most incredible example of generosity that anyone could ever imagine ... what you give to others unselfishly is utterly amazing.

Thanks for sharing your contagious love and excitement for learning, that taught us to appreciate the excellent educations you provided.

Thank you for supporting our individuality. And thank you for continually trying to let go, even when we made that even harder than it already is. No matter what, you'll always be our Mom and Dad, the two people we can always count on and turn to for hugs that comfort, and words that console.

Thanks for showing us the importance of saying "I'm sorry" and forgiveness. Our family truly is a most important aspect of our lives.

Thank you especially for showing us how to stand up for ourselves and expressing with conviction what we really believe, while never forgetting to have open minds - because there are two sides to everything.

Through it all, no parents could have made us more proud to be their daughters and sons. Our love and absolute respect for you go beyond what words express. Thank you so much.

We love you.

Carolyn   Patti xo   Theresa xoxo   Beth xo   Sean   Kevin xo

June 11, 1994

June 11, 1994

This was framed after being read at our 25th Anniversary Mass

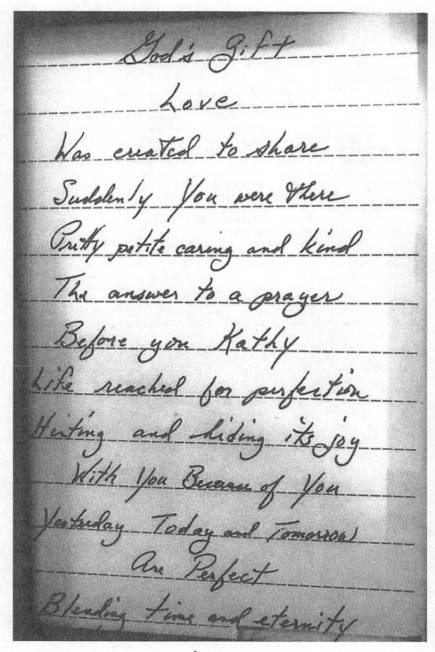

God's Gift
Love
Was created to share
Suddenly You were there
Pritty petite caring and kind
The answer to a prayer
Before you Kathy
Life reached for perfection
Hinting and hiding its joy
With You Because of You
Yesterday Today and Tomorrow
Are Perfect
Blending time and eternity

Just a note

Once again I recognize that I have travelled
down a road I did not choose.
In younger years I was intrigued by the road less travelled by
A poem penned to invite a different path I eagerly accepted
Thrilled and excited . . . I would again and again
say yes to a path.
Yet, more often still I find the road is not my selection
Never, never would I ask
Never, never would this be my selection
Swept along by the currents of wind, rain and storms of life
Life filled with happiness, love and beauty
Life created and carried by God's Hand
Life packed with imperfection
Imperfection, in personal pain
Pain persistent in spite of perseverance
Perseverance in pursuing illness
Chronic illness which steals life
Life, not just threatening death
but Life partly lived
Still filled with meaning . . .
with love . . . . with each other . . . . . with gratitude.
For a road never, never chosen
Painfully trod . . . . . peacefully accepted . . . today.
Embraced because it is ours.
Kathy and mine.
Thus it is invaluable.
It is ours.
Ours is wrapped in love
Imperfect, incomplete,
but real, true and fruitful
It takes us where it will . . . the destination out of sight
Sightless hand in hand we travel.
Toward each other, therefore to You
Thank you.

To my Kathy with all my
love Bob January 30, 2001

I penned this while sitting alone while Kathy was undergoing one
of her seventy-two cardiac catheterizations, It was taking too long.
I suspected a problem, She was defibrillated and survived.

Kathy and her friend made ditto's for school.

This reads
Mother as I have watched you live
as you believe, I have learned The meaning of Integrity

1991

Easter 2018
Kevin, Kathy Pete, Sean

Grandpa Poandl holding Joseph our first grandchild
Halloween 1991
I have my hand on our twins stroller Kevin and Sean

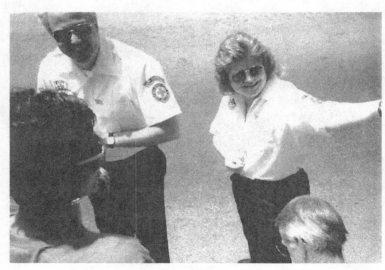

Memorial day parade 1991

Carolyn and Chris, Carolyn holding their son Joseph, Patti holding
Kevin, Theresa, Beth, Pete, Kathy holding Sean 1991.

Halloween 1999
3 months after stem cell transplant

Patti's graduation 1992

2006

Halloween 1996

Christmas parade 2012

As a gift of love and friendship, the Carmelites are remembering you and your intentions in five Novenas of Masses beginning on Christmas Day.

Christmas Season, 2018

Dear Dr. Freis and family,

May the infant Jesus touch your heart this Christmas with awe, wonder, and the gift of His unending love.

I think I can safely say that Dr. Freis personified love in many forms — wife, mother, grandmother, nurse, friend. May her love and example continue to radiate through all of you. And inspire the rest of us to be a little bit kinder in 2019.

Warmly,

Russ + Mary Anne, Tanya and Brendan + Mairéad

A Brief History of Lupus

*I*n the modern era of medicine, the health professionals understand and can address SLE more effectively. The nature and progression of SLE was beginning to be understood in the 1940s. It was not until then, after hundreds of years of effort, that medicine began to dimly illuminate the disease process through scientific inquiry and offer the suffering patient hope.

For many centuries before Christ, the disease was considered to be a skin disorder. This concept of a disease consisting solely of cutaneous lesions was a dense thicket of thought that was extremely slow to change. Hippocrates described its skin manifestations as herpes esthiomenos. In his era, there were many skin disorders because of inadequate hygiene and nutrition.

The use of Greek terms was continued after the fall of the Greek Empire. Multiple historical physicians continued to group cancer, infection, and lupus as one disorder. Rogerius, a physician in the 1300s, used the title *lupus* to describe facial lesions that resembled a wolf's bite.

Late in the nineteenth century, the understanding of lupus as a systemic disease was beginning. Internal organ involvement could occur without skin manifestations. The concept of its more devastating nature gradually gained acceptance. SLE is a disease which can virtually affect every organ of the body directly or indirectly.

The cause and progression of SLE was discovered in the late 1940s. At the same time, the availability of steroids and antimalarials were promising. Equally hopeful was the emergence of immunosuppressive therapy.

When lupus came to our home, Kathy and I called for help from many medical disciplines in our need. They responded well.

Meeting and More

We met when Kathy was working a weekend shift at Saint Peter's Hospital in New Brunswick, New Jersey. The hospital has been renamed Saint Peter's University Hospital because of its academic affiliations. She had recently started working on floor 5-D, a medical-surgical unit, after graduation from nursing school. Kathy was a new and very young registered nurse.

Fresh from an accelerated nursing program at Saint Francis School of Nursing in Trenton, New Jersey, she was twenty years old. Her nursing skills were mastered through a twenty-four-month program. She attended classes throughout the calendar year. The accelerated program provided her with an excellent education as a scholarship recipient.

Kathy was among the youngest in her class, and her peers told me she was among the brightest. Throughout her school years, she was always the youngest or almost so in each class. At age four, she started kindergarten at Saint Francis School in her hometown of Metuchen, New Jersey. Followed by attending Metuchen High School, her academic performance won her a full scholarship to nursing school. A person who cares for others is a perfect definition of Nurse Kathy. Nurse Kathy was an affectionate title bestowed on her by her patients. It was March 1967.

We met on a Saturday in mid-March 1967. I was a second-year medical school student. It happened that I needed to return home because of family illness.

The overnight train from Washington DC arrived in New Brunswick early Saturday morning. I was worried about my mother. On arrival at the hospital, I was pleased and relieved to see that my mother was recovering. I was a preclinical student steeped in science. I had yet to acquire the clinical skills I looked forward to.

My mother and I chatted. Adjacent to her bed rested pictures of her family. It was a common practice to have mementoes to remind the patient of home at that time. My mother told me that her nurse was very nice. I appreciated the kind words with which my mother described Kathy. I followed Mom's suggestion to meet her.

The short walk to the nurses' station changed my life. Just in front of me was a cute little blond. Wow!

Petite and pretty, she greeted me. This picture of her is still in my mind, as though it is happening now. Her crisp white uniform and cap, the uniform of that day, was perfect. She crouched and while she was peering into the desk she returned my hello.

Kathy was petite. She spoke softly and clearly in a caring considerate manner. She was lovely. There was a warm, good-natured way about her. I knew she was special.

Her pleasant manner was welcoming. She was very pretty. The day was instantly exciting! I hoped to get to know her.

On return to my studies, I tried to locate her. At first frustrated, my efforts were rewarded. My future sister-in-law attended the same elementary school and knew her. I called her.

Our first date was Holy Saturday, March 25, 1967. She had just celebrated her twenty-first birthday on March 16th. We enjoyed a movie Georgy Girl.

It was an hour's ride to the theater in Asbury Park, New Jersey. The movie was a little silly but popular at the time. Our enjoyment was getting to know each other while we drove to the shore.

We shared who we were. Kathy was the fourth of ten children. I was a twin with my brother. She had just started work and knew a little about me from my mother. I was eager to hear more about her. She enjoyed her family and her nursing.

Kathy was easy to be with and to talk to. Our conversation flowed the whole evening. She was also very patient.

On the long ride home, I was telling her in great detail about the research I would soon present at school. Kathy impressed me with her attentiveness. I rambled on as I drove. I admired the way she listened to my tale. The topic would be boring to most listeners. Years later, she told me she fell asleep after a hard day's work. That was okay with me. I was still pleased, very much so.

We attended midnight Mass because she had to work early the next morning. I can picture her beside me in church in her blue outfit. I planned to see her often. As the year passed, I did just that.

My dormitory was a converted apartment building that housed the law and medical students at George Washington University. Like other students, I took my turn at one of the few pay phones available. The circumstances met our needs measured in pennies, nickels, and dimes.

I called Kathy as often as possible. Her family had a party line, and we sometimes bumped into her neighbors by phone. They were nice people. Courtesy of the number of coins necessary to place a call, our phone visits were brief. The coming summer months allowed us to spend the time we wanted together.

She was the first girl I met who was a true Yankee fan. I followed the Yankees for years. The Yankees were her father's favorite team. He and I attended games together when I was in training and gained seats at the games in exchange for medical coverage.

As a first-year medical student, I had a demanding curriculum. Very eager to learn, I explained to Kathy that I may not be home for eight weeks. I hoped she would understand. She did.

Her patient understanding of my obligations was evident and most impressive to me. As a professional nurse, she knew better than I what medicine would demand. At that time, I was studying pre-clinical pathology and physiology. Next year, I would attend my first patient.

We took our studies seriously. As a nursing student at Saint Francis, the student was required to pass a nursing board examination. Kathy excelled and achieved the highest score in microbiology on her national nursing board examination that the experienced professor had ever witnessed. Throughout her lifetime, employed or volunteering, she continued her education and never relinquished her nursing license.

Just prior to our marriage, Kathy volunteered to provide nursing care to the poor of Appalachia. She worked with the Glenmary Home Missioners in the Smoky Mountains of North Carolina. There she went to homes and hospitals to care for the sick.

I visited once briefly over a weekend. It was truly obvious how especially well she was received and respected. The Glenmary Sisters loved her as did her patients. One home visit is singled out in memory.

On Sunday morning, Kathy and I visited a kind elderly gentleman at his home just to say hello. He, like many, was poor.

While I remained in the car, Kathy went to greet him on the porch of his home. It was a bright sunny morning. Their friendship was radiantly obvious. He, not much taller than her, was smiling and happy. He gave her an apple with his face glowing with gratitude. He received not only nursing care but gained a friend as well. Love is the basis for it all.

Her patient gave all that he had, his apple. The people of Appalachia were generous and appreciative of those who came to their home. Some homes were one room with three walls. In Hayesville, North Carolina, no one would pass you on the street without saying hello.

Kathy's nursing care was one of her gifts she offered to others. She gave her all. She gave herself. Her love was obvious. She was always happy to meet a stranger and included everyone.

Kathy was easy to be with. It is simply a pleasure to be with her. She brought joy to those around her through her gentle way as she smiled. She gave comfort to her patients and their family. Competency and caring were her gifts to her coworkers also. She comforted us because of our concern for her.

Whenever she arrived, she was enthusiastically welcomed. At every gathering, she chose to attend to others. Every courtesy, greeting, and sharing was done in a way that would boost the other person. She demonstrated how much she valued you and your relationship with her.

We spent more than fifty-two years together, at first getting to know and respecting each other, then to admire, appreciate, and love one another.

Nurse Kathy

*N*urse Kathy was the affectionate title given to Kathy by the children at Saint Cecilia's and Saint Francis School. She finished her professional career as a school nurse at these schools. These were demanding positions. Health screenings and everyday needs required near constant attention. All was accomplished with a smile.

Kathy accepted both nursing positions because she wanted to help her sisters. Carol was the nurse at Saint Cecilia's and Patricia was the nurse at Saint Francis. Both needed assistance. Kathy joined them. She enjoyed the kids, and they enjoyed her. Part of the fun of being at a school is getting to know everyone.

She was a school nurse, hospital nurse, and a visiting nurse for the Visiting Nurse Association. She traveled throughout the county to perform screenings and support the well-being of patients and their family. When possible, I would bring our boys and girls to have a quick lunch with Mommy.

While working at Saint Francis, Kathy expanded her presence by her helpful efforts in the classroom and school positions. She was a class mother and served two terms as home school copresident. Kathy was an EMT.

Our family volunteered on the town first-aid squad. Kathy was president, and we all rode the ambulance. Fundraisers and administration were essential to the squad and demanded her time and energy. Her response was outstanding.

She did not like speaking in public. These positions required it. In each position, she placed the mission before herself. She was a professional.

Kathy was my support to learn and then practice medicine. She was my helpmate as a husband and a father. Your spouse creates and provides you your home. She gives it warmth and inviting beauty. Her presence decorates the house with love, making it a home. Each child is indescribably beautiful and limitlessly lovable. Her love extended beyond our home.

Kathy was a remarkably knowledgeable, competent, and compassionate nurse whose bedside care was outstanding. I have often observed her healing touch, particularly with a terminally ill patient, with profound admiration. Her healing touch was a caress that completed each patient's care. It takes courage to address the trials of disease and death and turn them around. Clinical skills must be acquired and continually improved over a lifetime. You must always be a student for the benefit of the patient.

My family benefited from Kathy's skilled nursing care, she cared for my mother who returned to her home well. When we first met, I marveled at the interest Kathy had in the research I was conducting. Although exhausted, she understood fully the details of the work. She knew her biochemistry.

She left hospital work to join a Metuchen pediatric practice. She loved children. The practice was extremely busy and attended dozens of patients daily. In the summer, I would meet her after work. She was never disgruntled or dismayed by the workload. Energetic and pleased with her day's effort, we would enjoy our evening together. It was a great summer.

Kathy was the breadwinner the first year we were married. She worked at the George Washington University Hospital on a medical floor. We would part early in the morning when I followed my student clinical rotations. Happily we would meet during the day; and better still, we would work on the same floor when I rotated through medicine. It was good.

Nearly two years later, when she was in her third trimester of pregnancy and nearing her due date, we resuscitated a patient. We were first in the room and initiated the code 9. Airway established, we continued the patient's care successfully. That was not easy for a tiny very pregnant nurse. The patient did well.

Recently, out of curiosity, I asked Kathy if it was intimidating to transfer to a tertiary medical center after working in community hospitals. I reminded her that on her last day of work three days before giving birth, she cared for a bedside dialysis patient and another very sick man with insecticide poisoning.

She, in a matter-of-fact manner, simply stated that her singular worry was being the only nurse in charge of multiple personnel. Those working under her supervision were good supportive people. Just before going on maternity leave, they surprised her with a baby shower, after work. Kathy was well respected by her coworkers. They would complement her when they saw me. She supported their hard work. She was my bulwark.

One busy, exhausting overnight shift in a military hospital, I required assistance. I did not know the nurse working with me. While we worked, she shared that her husband was not successful in his goal of entering medical school. Her comments, spoken with feeling, were that she was pleased that he would not have demands placed on him like those we were addressing.

I was tired and frustrated. I told her that without my wife's support I would not be able to do this. This was a simple truthful statement. Your wife's support is the basis of that which you are capable of achieving.

At another duty station, we met again. I stepped out of my office and seated in the waiting room directly before me, I recognized the same nurse and her husband. I remembered very well that difficult night. Equally vivid was the sentiment she expressed. Her purpose in visiting me was to introduce her husband.

She was so pleased with my testimony to my wife and her support that she wanted us to meet. My statement was really Kathy's message—to give of yourself. Teach others to love.

Kathy put her values into action. Her values and ability to love were expressed in everything she did. She was wise and knew when not to intervene. This is a very difficult skill and not often seen.

Her love of God was why she could love me and love our family so well. She kept everyone close to each other in love. Her love reached beyond our family. She saw you and met you where you were.

Kathy made an effort to simplify difficulties. Quietly her words, manner, or calming silence facilitated solutions. In happy times, we purely enjoyed the moment. Its pleasure was portioned out for each to share and remember. Support was always there in the valleys of life.

Clarity of thought permits one because of its simplicity to achieve this. Her complete undistracted attention to the moment, the person, and the event gave value to all three. This was a gift. This gift showed her genuine goodness as a person and drew you to her.

She chose to love. This was a deliberate decision, and it was unchanging. She purposely cared lovingly for her family, her children, grandchildren, and extended family. Love is reciprocal. She constantly faced obstacles while putting her love in action because of her chronic illness. Her continuous effort was her prayer for us. We need to follow her example of how to love. In loving us, she loved God above all. She loved selflessly and completely. Your wife gives you your life, family, and friends. How we do things matters.

Kathy made what was important to us important to her. She very carefully weighed all of the decisions we made as husband and wife. We mutually chose what was best as we made our way through life. She made us first in her heart and thoughts in everything.

She spoke her mind and did so considerately and clearly. Her honesty made burdensome decisions lighter. We did well, and worries became opportunities. Persistence paid well. We were a good match. We were a team. Family was always first.

My wife's ability to love was evident every minute of her life. I learned from her. She influenced people. She participated in their lives and made their lives better. This made Kathy attractive. She accepted you.

A nursing school classmate who was close to Kathy told me about a retreat they attended. The theme of the retreat was being Christ to others. After the session, she told me Kathy was Christ to her, and she would never forget her.

While loving and caring for others, Kathy did not neglect her own needs. She vigorously pursued health. We were athletic. As a kid, she enjoyed running. She jogged with me and the kids. Our nutrition was excellent. "Feed them, and they will come," is a famous quote from her. It is repeated often in family circles. In spite of dreadful, threatening disease, Kathleen skillfully mastered multiple roles throughout her life.

These accomplishments are because Kathy put her love into practice. All of her relationships were caring, compassionate, and respectful. She was nonjudgmental and always accepting of the other person.

Relationships of this quality grow. The individual will grow as a person, and the relationship will blossom. Families will truly care for each other and thrive.

During the last week of her life, Kathy softly repeated "please, please." I then thought she was requesting help. Before surgery, she told me how much she wanted to live for our grandchildren. I supported her with all my heart and my entire being.

In response to her, "please," I reassured her that she was getting help. That was true at the time. The team of providers were attentive to every detail as was I.

Today I wonder if her petition may also mean continue her message. Love one another and forgive one another. Be accepting of each other. There are no exceptions.

Patience and the ability to simplify the difficult were among her many virtues and beauty. They were her gifts that she shared with us all. She wanted to continue to live for us. She lived the life God gave her. A gift from Him returned to Him when she exhausted every breath and all the strength she had.

It would be wise to continue what she taught us, to continue to influence others for their betterment, simply to love one another.

Christmas Trees

*C*hristmas trees are very important in our family. Kathy and I started a tradition. Each tree was chosen with care to bring its majesty into our home. We selected very large magnificent and full Douglas Fir trees to last the entire Christmas season and longer.

Before we were married, Kathy and I persuaded her family to go to a tree farm to cut their own Christmas tree. During the exciting Christmas season, the Poandl living room was filled with a tree that reached to the ceiling. It was always a big tree. A beautiful brightly shining angel crowned the tree. Presents, our large family and friends surrounded the tree. Multiple generations gathered underneath its boughs. We made the fun last as long as possible.

Fresh cut and perfectly placed in a cool formal living room in our home, each tree was radiant. Each ornament found its special branch. If made or given by one of the children, they placed their masterpiece on the tree. Christmas after Christmas, the tree would win the title of the best Christmas tree ever. When the tree was fully decorated, with every branch full, this title was announced. All the kids of all ages expected the award.

We put so much effort into selecting, transporting, and decorating the trees we were reluctant to take them down. On arrival at our home, it could require the help of three sturdy strong people to bring it inside. Once placed properly, it took hours to put the lights on. Each step had to be just right. The crowd, our kids, and their families, assembled. We made the most of the Christmas-tree decorating. Grandma's delicious homemade vegetable soup kept us going. Kathy continued to make it from scratch when Grandma went to heaven. This year, we followed the same recipe when Kathy went to heaven. Delicious food always added to the delight of the family on most occasions.

The ornaments came from many generations with new contributions each year. On Saint Nicholas Day (December Six), each child or grandchild found an ornament nestled in their shoe placed at the doorstep. The decoration would reflect in its theme the child's interests. The sport or activity, a baseball or acrobat, displayed by the trinket clearly told you who the treasure belonged to. Some of the decorations were old treasures from the grandparents with fond memories. Others from friends demonstrated their closeness and how well we knew each other. Coworkers and patients said thank you with creative little nurses and doctors. Each of the children were given a chest of decorations special to them to grace the homes they would create as adults.

Long lived, the Christmas trees became Valentine's Day trees by changing the lights to red and white. Red paper hearts were added by our then little girls. The trees were carefully tended and could live for months. Years ago, one of our sons-in-law marveled at a tree still standing in March.

Reluctantly, each tree became a featherweight and went its way. We needed to make room for future family celebrations. Before saying goodbye, we would have a Christmas tree picnic. Our crowd would contribute summer fare for the feast, hamburgers, salads, and desserts for us to share once more. These traditions continue to grow and will be long remembered. We did not stop with Valentine's Day.

Saint Patrick's Day made everything green. Easter blossomed in purple, pink, and yellow trim. All birthdays, spring and fall, brought a festive atmosphere and us all home. We came home to enjoy and celebrate each other. This renewed who we are.

It is important that you know Kathy. She was able to not allow disappointment get in the way. We started off simply and moved frequently.

Our Arlington third floor apartment showed off our first Christmas tree the December after we married. My baby daughter and I went off to our parish, Saint John's, to carefully select the perfect tree. I was literally on my own.

Proud of my selection, I stood next to the car while Kathy looked from the third-floor window. I displayed my prize. The tree was in one hand and Carolyn in my arm. Kathy seemed to marvel at my choice of a tree. She was being most kind. She always was. The tree was really bare and far from magnificent. When I see it in old pictures, I wonder what I was thinking. All Christmas trees in her family were full and stretched to the ceiling. I resolved that all Christmas trees would be bigger, better, fuller, and more beautiful.

Each year, we chose our trees more carefully. One tree was so large I removed five feet of its trunk to place it in the living room. We were then stationed in the army with quarters which had ten-foot high ceilings. At this post, Kathy won the award for best Christmas decorations in family housing. Our first few years of marriage were nomadic.

We lived in several states and made do with the housing available for us. Some choices were limited by location, others by what we could afford. We measured our trees with a yardstick determined by where we were. Perhaps the Christmas trees were an assessment of where we were. We loved being married. The Christmas tree adventures of the Freis family is a sample of that joy.

Every holiday was jubilant!

Family

*K*athy expressed her message of love through her family. She was a loving, caring child and sister. Her uncles told me how much they enjoyed her. Her Uncle Joe used to sing "K-A-T-I-E" as soon as he saw her. He still did years later. My memory of her sharing the swings with her sister, as a young boy, is telling to me. They were playing in a lush green yard, their blond hair glistening in the sun, the same yard that Kathy and I would play with our children and grandchildren on the same swing set.

The Christmas just before we were married conveys a beautiful memory of her. We both grew up in homes with hard-working parents and limited financial resources. She earned her nursing education through a full scholarship to an accelerated program, twelve continuous months a year, at Saint Francis Nursing School. Her first employment at Saint Peter's Hospital started promptly. She was overjoyed to be able for the first time to purchase Christmas presents with more freedom.

She laughed and giggled as we shopped and returned to her house with the treasures. I remember standing on the front steps and asking her about the cost of the gifts. She was exuberant when she explained that this was the first time she could give *nice* gifts. She never stopped giving. She constantly gave of herself.

Christmas today continues in the manner in which she would express the holiday, in faith and love. She surprised me with her presents.

I did not know what she had done prior to her November surgery for pancreatic adenocarcinoma. This was the disease that she could not survive. The cancer enveloped intestinal blood vessels that had to be removed to excise the tumor. This left Kathy dependent for life on vessels severely diseased years ago by systemic lupus erythematosus. We could not know this without the necessary surgery.

This fall 2018, while I was at work, she and our daughter Beth were organizing our bedroom. There were bags of Christmas and birthday presents to collect, wrap, and distribute. Kathy had been in the process of readying all the Christmas gifts. I continue to see many examples of my wife's effort to spare us. I am very grateful for her selfless love throughout our more than fifty-two years together.

Christmas was one of her favorite holidays. She anticipated gifts for family and friends months before. The just right gift for someone would be purchased and secreted away. I usually assisted in the plans. This year, we were well stocked with presents for everyone.

A most special gift she gave our entire family was to reunite everyone. Like my family, some ill-defined discord gauged a rift in relationships. My own close family, who gathered most Sunday evenings and visited often, drifted apart during my teenage years. My youth simply did not equip me to assemble the pieces of the puzzle together.

Kathy did much better than I. She was superb in her fantastic party planning and its enduring sweeping success. Once reunited, the family remained close.

As our children grew and reached seven years old, we anticipated their first Holy Communion. This sacrament is usually received in the spring; but in our home, the children's First Holy Communion followed right after Christmas.

We planned a huge celebration in our home. Every member of the family, near and far, was invited. We cooked for one solid week. It took the entire week to prepare all the yummy dishes. Self-proclaimed chefs offered special treats. Decorations expanded, and enthusiasm grew over the years for Aunt Kathy's parties. We had the good fortune to have Uncle Bob home for the holidays.

Uncle Bob was a missionary who brought the Gospel to rural poor. He returned home each Christmas. He offered Mass, First Penance, and First Holy Communion to our children and grandchildren.

The combination of the holidays and the sacraments bonded us all. This was real family. A crowd of ordinary people, who loved one another, just as a family should. It was great. The results were lifelong and present today.

The best part was getting to know each other. Kathy and I invited dozens of people to our home. It was incredible.

Kathy did this quietly and lovingly with her welcoming smile. We were exhausted and happy. Feed them she did by serving plentiful scrumptious meals. Her frequent and plentiful dinners were impromptu or by invitation or on the occasion of someone or something to honor.

Two great feasts were Halloween and Easter. Two very different holidays; but in our house, a crowd assembled for food, fun, and fond memories. Laughter was the music, and the mood was joyful.

One of our younger grandchildren would respond German macaroni when Halloween was mentioned. Skip the candy. This dish was a family favorite and a labor of love. Our large family and their friends would rendezvous at our house between candy-seeking excursions around the neighborhood. When parents came to our door, a sometimes request for German macaroni was made.

A huge pot of Kathy's original recipe for German Macaroni would simmer available for all, including a few trick-or-treaters who were wise to our ways. Six pounds of pasta later, all were satiated and grinning ear to ear. All of us were in some silly costume.

We chose our costumes carefully and embellished them in any imaginable way. We were soldiers, celebrities, bubble-gum machines, and M&Ms candy. All went home contented at the end of the memorable day. Future feasts with the ghosts and goblins were promised and anticipated.

Our nieces and nephews remembered Aunt Kathy's parties happily. In fact, they were reported to be the best parties ever.

Easter was the favorite. Preparations for Easter seemed to go on forever. Dozens and dozens of eggs were dyed. Corsages and flower arrangements were handmade. Favorite breads and pies arrived for Easter.

As Lent came to a conclusion, we attended services on Holy Thursday and Good Friday. Our food for Easter Sunday was blessed early Holy Saturday. Then egg-coloring filled the rest of Saturday afternoon. We ate.

Early Easter morning, we joined together again for the first of several Easter egg hunts. Multiple pictures were taken of us dressed in our finery in our decorated yard. The trees were adorned with brightly colored eggs. Bunnies popped from flower pots but kept the eggs location secret. The little Easter bunny was considered to be very clever in his choice of out-of-sight spots.

Easter Mass was followed by a true feast which lasted into the evening. The lively spirit of the day was embraced by the family.

Family fun was explosive. Easter baskets, pretty dresses, handsome suits were all dressed perfectly with smiles. The earliest Easter egg hunt was at our home. The second was at the sprawling yard at 443, Grandma's and Grandpa's home. Dinner followed.

Lamb and ham and trimmings were passed around the dining room table. Food then went to the TV room and was passed to the left. Additional folding tables and chairs were added to accommodate the ninety-plus guests at table. Happily, more family joined us later for dessert. There was always room.

As our family grew, we enlarged our home. We extended the back of our house followed by a second addition to the side of the first. A very detailed goal of our planning was to include everyone at our table for Easter. We succeeded. Kathy encouraged company, "If you feed them, they will come." They did. What you do matters.

Relationships

Successful relationships require effort. Kathy knew this well. She recognized the other person for who they were. She assessed how to meet their needs. She also knew how to share these skills. How? Kathy was observant.

We were in the car one day, an ordinary day on which we were traveling back and forth on simple errands. Seated to my right, her tone and posture were purposeful. She quietly shared she knew how difficult it must be to meet our family's financial needs. The demands were troubling at the time. She softly said in her beautiful way she appreciated my efforts.

Most importantly, out of her wisdom, couched in love, she offered that one person cannot fully understand another person's burden. I consumed what she said and saved it for the treasure her advice was.

Her witness to my concerns at the moment and many other times was affirming. Kathy was most aware of another's emotions and needs. Without great detail, her simple council refocused my thinking. A better perspective and attitude straightens the road while it eases the burden.

The acquisition of social and emotional wisdom gives order to life. To share this wisdom is to love someone. Wisely pursued and offered, insight permits you to love and be loved. It must be practiced and honed to achieve. It is unselfish.

These social skills demand paying attention to a person and attentiveness to the details of another's demeanor, word, and action. You must choose to be patient. Quick or rash judgement must be put aside.

Kathy's mother conspicuously displayed a banner which read, "Grow where you are planted" (1 Corinthians 7:20–24). When I first saw it as a young man, I did not appreciate its wisdom. Mulled over repeatedly in my mind, its message became meaningful. God's wisdom placed you in a fertile field where you can grow best, best as a person and in relationships where your talents can be best used, the best place for you in time and eternity.

The ability to love was handed down to Kathy and her siblings by the example of her parents, Dorothy and Frank. The children benefited from the home atmosphere. They grew well. The home is the best school.

Wisdom

*W*isdom takes many forms. We might expect to hear wise words from a public speaker or in a classroom, perhaps in a house of worship.

Wisdom might be expected in the resolution of a difficult decision or simply demonstrated by a manner of behavior by just joining in the moment, be it washing dishes, taking out the garbage, or cleaning up after a gathering. It can be heard when laughter echoes or a cause for concern is expressed.

Be a part of whatever it is. Togetherness is the reward. A note honoring Kathy and her brother Bob says this well. It expresses love and appreciation for them both. Ann recognizes Kathy's wisdom.

Everyday people make most of life happen doing everyday things. The day is full of cooking, cleaning, homework, gardening, shopping, errands, repairs, drop off, and pickup of spouses and children, business, and pleasure.

Dreary or fun and exciting days pack our lives. Each day can get away from us as time moves along.

We have so many common experiences and roles. How we live and share these events and relationships enhances us as individuals. Most importantly, these enhance those we share life with.

Kathy mastered this value and lived it.

February 2019

Dear Pat & Jerry, Pete & Family, Tom & Deb, Dave & Pam, Ed & Diane, Christine & Yasser, Bill & MaryBeth,

At the repast for Bob, my heart felt both broken and lifted up. The stories about Bob were very touching. As many family members and friends mentioned, Bob truly listened and made an impact on every person he met. Back in 1983, I spent a week in Georgia helping the Sisters in Bob's parish. I could see the mutual devotion and respect between Bob and his parishioners. I also witnessed Bob's great devotion to your incredible Mom and family with the speed in which he was able to return to Metuchen when she passed away that week.

I experienced Bob's healing powers when I tagged along on one of his trips into NYC with a few lucky nieces and nephews. My back had been bothering me a bit on the ferry trip over, and when we started walking towards Battery Park, it became so painful that I planned to take the ferry back home right away so as not to ruin the trip for anyone. We stopped in a nearby church which held the Shrine of St. Elizabeth Ann Seton. While I was sitting near the Shrine, Bob asked to rest his hand on my back. I believe we sat there for about 5 minutes. When I stood up, my back pain was completely gone. I have never forgotten Bob's healing presence that day.

Your brother lived God's Word by sharing his love, healing, kindness, joy, and laughter to those he met. I imagine he changed many lives and hearts during his long, difficult years at Butner. I feel blessed and humbled to have him in my life.

I also want to honor Kathy and her welcoming smiles, humble manner, endless support and love for her family and friends, dedication to children—small and tall, and quick wit. I was amazed at her strength while facing each new battle. A fond memory I have of Kathy is that, no matter whose house it was, I would find her helping in the kitchen, especially washing the dishes, which (I only just figured out) enabled her to chat with just about everyone since we all ended up in the kitchen eventually—so, so wise.

What a blessing to have shared time with Bob and Kathy. I keep your family in my prayers.

Love to all,

Ann

Let People Love You

*L*et people love you. One of the people Kathy befriended over the years was because of her warm smile. When the individual came to our town, Kathy smiled at her after church. My wife was among the first to greet her. Subsequently we enjoy the monthly home delivery of a delicious Irish soda bread.

The smile was shared as a simple gesture while leaving church, a fleeting smile that touched a stranger's heart. That is all it takes. Kathy knew this, and it was a part of her way of life.

So many families are broken. So many people are broken. Parents and siblings do not speak to each other. Years go by. Separation widens, and death occurs without reconciliation. This is fixable.

Let people love you. Opportunities are missed daily to say, "I love you," in word, action, or purposeful silence. These opportunities permit you to grow. Sometimes the spoken word can be replaced with a whispered prayer. "Say it in prayer," was the advice in a homily preached some time ago. It is good advice and allows time or another day for the recipient of the lover to accept the gift of their affection.

So many times an offer to reconcile is dismissed or rebuked with anger. Emotions determine our behavior so frequently in countless ways. Defenses and avoidance, misunderstanding, or some other obstacle intrudes. Let it go. Please let it go.

Letting someone love you is an active process. It is a decision. It can be chosen. It may require an evaluation of who, what, and where you are. Sometimes it demands letting go of hurt, actually pausing to let the storm pass. It is a process with choices and consequences, some of which are not wanted. It forces an evaluation of priorities. It requires vulnerability. It demands humility and selflessness. Letting someone close requires understanding, compassion, and empathy. These attributes must be put into action.

Priorities can, in love, define the responses. Priorities can permit patience and its rewards to prevail. Saint Therese's prayer says, "Patience obtains all things." Time may need to pass.

Kathy valued the person so highly and so well that they tried to imitate her. I admired how beautifully she did this. Initiating a conversation with someone can soften or avoid a confrontation if carefully worded. A gentle affirmation of a sensitive feeling or issue without criticism was a gentle, meaningful step forward. Defenses were dropped, walls torn down, and relationships nourished through her. Her patience, her choice to endure pain or conflict allowed her to always love. How valuable a lesson she taught just by being herself.

Kathy did not allow the hurt inflicted by another in any way, great or small, divert her from reaching out to another. Her intent was to love. Her personal pain was not an impediment. Her disease did not stop her. She did this in a gentle, quiet manner. She did this without exception.

If rejected, her effort never ceased. Quietly, gently, the relationship was carefully healed. Rebuilt brick by brick, a new structure heralded the future, the restructuring of the broken bonds. She loved even though she was in pain.

Letting someone love you is not submission. It is not giving in or always agreeing. Emotions linger after decisions are made regardless of their depth or quality. To disagree is not to reject a person. It is a wonderful way to affirm the truth and open up to each other.

So How Do We Love One Another?

This is one important question. It is essential to a relationship, especially marriage.

We can

Learn to love.

Appreciate each other for who we are, what we do, say, and not mention.

Be grateful—express your gratitude as often as possible.

Be humble. We and life are not perfect. Place your spouse before you. Trust your spouse in everything. Your needs are important to your mate.

Make what is important to your spouse important to you.

Be patient—always.

Keep promises, especially the little ones. Be predictable. Your spouse counts on you. Always tell the truth.

If anything or anyone interferes with your relationship, step far, far away. Forgive, easily done when you imitate God's forgiveness. Forgive and forget. Hold hands.

Take walks alone together.

Plan. Our plans will change but plan together anyway. Have children. They promise the future—busy, imperfect but real.

Our children assist in our own development and learning how to love.

Love your children unconditionally. They are part of you.

Be kind always.

Be a likeable you. Your family needs you to be so.

Work very, very hard. It is essential.

Play just as hard. This brings everyone closer together.

KATHY'S WAY

Laugh often. This brings joy.
If ill or hurt, make it a prayer, imitating Jesus.
God comes first.
Thank you, Kathy, for showing me how.

Keep Your Promises

*P*romises are important. Promises kept are very important. A pledge to another engenders expectation and is fostered by trust. It empowers people to pursue goals, perform well, and earn the respect and gratitude of the person to whom the promise is made.

Promises take many forms. Promises are big and small. Simple statements to assure another that an agreement will be honored. They take many forms. For example:

Legal contracts

Pay for work

Good grades for academic achievement

An assurance of your effort

Attendance at a meeting

A date planned

Confirmation of employment

Competence in your profession

Candidate platforms

The assurance of a promise can be moral, legal, or sacred. It binds one to perform. It is a bond between people.

Promises kept are worthy of respect. A person who keeps their promises is admired. This is a quality of great merit.

There are many kinds of people. A huge diversification of personalities, cultures, and traditions meet in families and individuals. All combine to create the person you are.

People

People

People come in many varieties. A local community today can easily be a global community. Through ancestry, our heritage and culture define us. Culturalization modifies and blends traditions and people.

The courtesy and care for each other expressed in respectful ways has been our experience throughout our lives. Regardless of individual traits, people and persons demonstrate their goodness. High moral character, empathy, sympathy, and consideration is commonplace.

Genuine concern for others is prevalent. Lifelong experience has repeatedly taught this lesson. Generosity has its rewards. Good people seek goodness. There are scores of good people.

Kathy enjoyed her friends and family. She was a people person. She was surrounded by genuine and enjoyable persons, many, many girls and guys who were a pleasure to be with.

Her family was welcoming, and we enjoy each other still. There was always someone or something to celebrate, an accomplishment or birthday, a graduation or a new cousin to make the day happy. Her friends welcomed you, and they were immediately your friend as well.

Everyone worked hard. Everyone played with gusto. From pinochle to baseball, swimming or camping, something was always going on.

The activity energized you and encouraged, inviting more to come. That atmosphere was pervasive and promising, a pledge of happiness that was astonishing. The promise was kept.

Kathy always kept her promises. Promises are essential to us all. We believe them. We trust them. We trust those who make them. We expect the fruit of the promise.

Our many years together, we, like most, knew the value of a promise kept. It is beautiful to hear the young couple reciting their wedding vows in public. The beautiful pledge of fidelity and love is indescribable. The trust in each other for a lifetime is matchless. The now defines who they are and who they will be.

Likewise, a simple promise of much less magnitude opens expectation. Expectation that the promise will be kept—a certitude that is reassuring, comforting, and peace giving, a comfort and peace built on the knowledge of promises kept, a trust in the person making the promise.

I knew very quickly the many attributes that Kathy possessed. I grew to know, trust, and love her. The many couples we know in our family and among our friends and colleagues are inspiring. Love given and received is indescribably wonderful beyond words.

When we exchanged our vows, Kathy spoke after me. With all my heart and affection, I recited after the priest, Uncle Bob, my vows in a crowded St. Francis Church. She, her beautiful eyes fixed on mine, told me her vows, before God, to me from her heart. She did not recite them. I am still in awe.

On our twenty-fifth wedding anniversary, I spontaneously renewed my vows at the celebratory Mass and party in imitation of her. She beautifully did the same. We repeatedly renewed our vows in special places, the site of the marriage feast in Cana and in St. Joseph's Chapel at the Guadalupe shrine. Even as Kathy neared death, we renewed our vows.

To love completely and to give of yourself is a most wonderful life. That is the wedding vow.

Little things add up. The everyday kindness, the respect for differing viewpoints, and understanding when things are not quite right add up. Honesty and respect allow different opinions and perspectives to play out well. Actually, these tools shape the fabric that clothes a relationship. They heal hurt and disappointment and reunite any fracture or wound. A promise fulfilled expresses love.

Love is expressed in a multitude of ways. Living life confirms this. Raising a family confirms this. Everything is gained by learning to love. The good in what is unable to be foreseen is gained through the trust of a promise kept.

Our Fiftieth Wedding Anniversary

*O*ur family gathered together at a seashore resort, a beautiful home, to celebrate our fiftieth wedding anniversary. The weekend was planned before Kathy's unexpected death in November. All of our children came to show their love and appreciation for Kathy and me. We accommodated six families easily. Our children are admirable for their inexhaustible enthusiasm for giving. Every detail mirrored Kathy's example of living for others.

When we arrived, my son and I strolled to the ocean's edge to be met by a much gentler February wind and wave than I expected. The dunes were broad and magnificent in spite of winter.

Each of our four daughters and their families arrived later. My other son arrived after work. It was too late past sunset to repeat our stroll then, but we did the following evening. The beach showed us dunes and ocean to the north and the skyline of a brightly blazing Atlantic City south of us. It was beyond wonderful to feel and observe their affection for each other. It was a good place to be. I was with everyone Kathy gave me. They gave me their love.

Dinners were planned and prepared to satisfy the heart, as well as the appetite. From pasta to savory roast pork, each dish was accompanied by equally delicious side dishes. We ate and played.

We played games and cards. No winners or losers. We chatted, laughed, crunched seashells as we walked the beach. My granddaughter reminded me that "Grandma is here." We had fun. Family is everything. In the sacrament of matrimony, you do become one.

This is Kathy's legacy, her gift to us. Love one another. Find a way to love one another. When a family comes together and grows closer, life cannot be better.

Our grandson Kyle wrote the following essay about his grandmother as part of his high school cultural identity project. Kyle beautifully related his grandmother's love for him. He also taught, as did she, how to love.

My Grandmother
Kyle Blom

Since the minute I was born into this world at 1:42 a.m. on November 1st, 2003, I have been nurtured and cared for by my grandma. The lessons that she has taught me have helped to mold me into the young man I am today. This amazing woman is Kathy Freis. She has taught me valuable life lessons, and I am so thankful for the role this beautiful lady has had in my life.

To begin, my grandma, Kathy Freis, has always taken special care of me. Since my infancy, she has always had a significant place in my well being. For instance, she gave me my first bath when I was a newborn, as was her tradition with all her grandchildren. She was also my first babysitter, when Mom went to work. Besides the loving care she administered, all through my baby years, she taught me lessons throughout my childhood. One of the most important teachings that my brothers and I were taught by Grandma was table manners. I remember one specific night, at Grandma's house, when she gave us a long talking to. Specifically, for me, it was about pushing the food onto my fork with my fingers while eating. With concern about my social etiquette, my Grandma quickly, but kindly, corrected this for me. Besides the teaching of table manners, my grandmother also created most of the traditions our family has always had for the holidays. She wanted the family to be close, all the time, but the holidays were especially important. My grandma wanted everyone present, for every event, that took place in her house. Thus, she would go to great lengths to ensure the plans were set in place, and everyone knew. Once the plans were made, she worked to make them happen. Easter is a perfect illustration of Grandma's diligence. Prior to our feast each year, you could always see her in her kitchen peeling, slicing and preparing the twenty pounds of scalloped potatoes, until sweat beaded on her forehead. In fact, seeing Grandma and Grandpa passed out on the coach or the floor from pure exhaustion was always as much a part of the yearly experience as egg hunting or eating candy. However, with this grit and resolve to celebrate, as a family, Grandma taught again. This time the lesson was FAMILY. To Grandma, her family was first, always first, and she made sure each one of us felt her love. Through her sleepless pre-holiday nights to ensure all details were taken care of, she taught through example. But, the greatest lesson that Grandma taught me was to take time. Take time to be with those you love. Grandma and I had a special tradition. After school, or when I just wanted to talk, she and I would snuggle and chat. She always made time for me, and always listened. In fact, sometimes she was the first person I would tell when something important or exciting happened. For me, everyday, Grandma was a constant: a constant teacher, a constant listener, a constant snuggler, a constant source of love.

On November 17, 2018, my grandma, Kathy Freis died. This was a huge blow not only for me as an individual, but for my family as a whole. Her death directly changed the way that my family was run. It was like taking out the engine of a vehicle. The person who ran the show was no longer here. For a while my family just "went through the motions" of daily life. For myself it lead to a downward spiral in my academic success, and I struggled for two months after her death. Besides the daughtening realization that this was our new reality, I also noticed my brothers and I had no one to keep us in line at the dinner table and my family had no one to add meaning and an agenda to the holidays. Yet, the thing that I really missed the most, and continue to miss everyday, is going over to Grandma's house, lying on her coach and snuggling with her. This time, when I would tell her about my day and the mistakes and the triumphs I made, was one of the highlights of my daily life. The loss of this special time with just Grandma and I leaves a huge hole in my heart.

Today, almost 5 months later, I understand Grandma's teachings even more, and her presence is amazingly palpable. I know and remember the teachings of being a gentleman with manners. My family, as a whole, remembers the important lesson of being together and being a loving family. For instance, although our first Christmas without Grandma was tough, her spirit was there as we carried out our Christmas traditions as we always had. In fact, my grandma shopped throughout the year for Christmas for us. She was always taking advantage of a "good deal". So, when during our gift exchange on Christmas Eve it was time for Grandpa to pass out his gifts, he went around the room and said to each grand-

child, including me, "This is from both of us."
Grandma had picked out most of our gifts. It was
a very tough holiday without Grandma, yet each
member of my family made an effort to be there,
and really celebrate what she gave us, each other.
With her in our hearts we powered through and
did all the things that she so precisely showed
us to do. Grandma gave us traditions. Grandma
gave us love.

My grandma, Kathy Freis, gave me gifts.
She taught me lessons that make me who I am
today. She helped me create an identity that
includes being a gentleman, an individual who
values family and tradition, and a young man
who understands the importance of pausing for a
hug and a chat. I miss her dearly, and I am trying
my best to carry out her lessons everyday. I know
that I am not and will not be perfect, yet I do live
by all the ideals she taught me, especially the one
thing she asked of me in her final hours on this
earth... Be kind.

About the Author

I am a pediatrician who has contributed to medical literature over his nearly fifty years of practice and teaching. The purpose of writing Kathy's Way is to share how one person, who by being herself, can change the world. Her message must continue.

CPSIA information can be obtained
at www.ICGtesting.com
Printed in the USA
BVHW030315110420
577308BV00023B/116